Monthly Planner

Mon	Tue	Wed	Thu

Fri	Sat	Sun	Note

Monthly Planner

Mon	Tue	Wed	Thu

Fri	Sat	Sun	Note

Monthly Planner

Mon	Tue	Wed	Thu

Fri	Sat	Sun	Note

Monthly Planner

Mon	Tue	Wed	Thu

Fri	Sat	Sun	Note

Monthly Planner

Mon	Tue	Wed	Thu

Fri	Sat	Sun	Note

Monthly Planner

Mon	Tue	Wed	Thu

Fri	Sat	Sun	Note

Monthly Planner

Mon	Tue	Wed	Thu

Fri	Sat	Sun	Note

Monthly Planner

Mon	Tue	Wed	Thu

Fri	Sat	Sun	Note

Monthly Planner

Mon	Tue	Wed	Thu

Fri	Sat	Sun	Note

Monthly Planner

Mon	Tue	Wed	Thu

Fri	Sat	Sun	Note

Monthly Planner

Mon	Tue	Wed	Thu

Fri	Sat	Sun	Note

Monthly Planner

Mon	Tue	Wed	Thu

Wedding Checklists

Wedding Checklists

Wedding Checklists

Wedding Checklists

Wedding Checklists

Wedding Checklists

Wedding Checklists

Wedding Ideas

Ideas

Note

Wedding Ideas

Ideas

Note

Wedding Ideas

Ideas

Note

Wedding Ideas

Ideas

Note

Budget Planner

Total Budget: ______________________

Categories & Details	Budget Cost	Actual Cost	Balance	Note

Budget Planner

Total Budget: ____________________

Categories & Details	Budget Cost	Actual Cost	Balance	Note

Budget Planner

Total Budget: ____________________

Categories & Details	Budget Cost	Actual Cost	Balance	Note

Budget Planner

Total Budget: ____________________

Categories & Details	Budget Cost	Actual Cost	Balance	Note

Budget Planner

Total Budget: ______________________

Categories & Details	Budget Cost	Actual Cost	Balance	Note

Budget Planner

Total Budget: ______________________

Categories & Details	Budget Cost	Actual Cost	Balance	Note

Pre-Wedding Details

Details

Note

To Do List

- ○
- ○
- ○
- ○
- ○
- ○
- ○
- ○
- ○
- ○
- ○
- ○
- ○

Pre-Wedding Details

Details

Note

To Do List

Wedding Day Schedule

Time	Event	Note

Wedding Day Schedule

Time	Event	Note

Wedding Speech

Note:

Wedding Speech

Note:

Wedding Speech

Note:

Wedding Speech

Note:

Bridal Shower

Details

Activity & Games

Food & Drink

Guest List

Name	Invitation

To Do List

- ○
- ○
- ○
- ○
- ○
- ○
- ○
- ○
- ○
- ○
- ○
- ○
- ○

Bridal Shower

Details

Activity & Games

Food & Drink

Guest List

Name	Invitation

To Do List

- ○
- ○
- ○
- ○
- ○
- ○
- ○
- ○
- ○
- ○
- ○
- ○
- ○

Bachelorette Party

Details

Schedule

Guest List

Name	Invitation

To Do List

- ○
- ○
- ○
- ○
- ○
- ○
- ○
- ○
- ○
- ○
- ○
- ○
- ○

Bachelorette Party

Details

Schedule

Guest List

Name	Invitation

To Do List

- ○
- ○
- ○
- ○
- ○
- ○
- ○
- ○
- ○
- ○
- ○
- ○
- ○

After Party

Details

Activity & Games

Food & Drink

Guest List

Name	Invitation

To Do List

- ○
- ○
- ○
- ○
- ○
- ○
- ○
- ○
- ○
- ○
- ○
- ○
- ○

After Party

Details

Activity & Games

Food & Drink

Guest List

Name	Invitation

To Do List

- ○
- ○
- ○
- ○
- ○
- ○
- ○
- ○
- ○
- ○
- ○
- ○
- ○

Guest Lists

Name	Address	Phone	Status		
			Invited	RSVP	Thankyou
			☐	☐	☐
			☐	☐	☐
			☐	☐	☐
			☐	☐	☐
			☐	☐	☐
			☐	☐	☐
			☐	☐	☐
			☐	☐	☐
			☐	☐	☐
			☐	☐	☐
			☐	☐	☐
			☐	☐	☐
			☐	☐	☐
			☐	☐	☐
			☐	☐	☐
			☐	☐	☐
			☐	☐	☐
			☐	☐	☐
			☐	☐	☐
			☐	☐	☐
			☐	☐	☐
			☐	☐	☐
			☐	☐	☐
			☐	☐	☐
			☐	☐	☐
			☐	☐	☐

Guest Lists

Name	Address	Phone	Status		
			Invited	RSVP	Thankyou
			☐	☐	☐
			☐	☐	☐
			☐	☐	☐
			☐	☐	☐
			☐	☐	☐
			☐	☐	☐
			☐	☐	☐
			☐	☐	☐
			☐	☐	☐
			☐	☐	☐
			☐	☐	☐
			☐	☐	☐
			☐	☐	☐
			☐	☐	☐
			☐	☐	☐
			☐	☐	☐
			☐	☐	☐
			☐	☐	☐
			☐	☐	☐
			☐	☐	☐
			☐	☐	☐
			☐	☐	☐
			☐	☐	☐
			☐	☐	☐
			☐	☐	☐
			☐	☐	☐

Guest Lists

Name	Address	Phone	Status		
			Invited	RSVP	Thankyou
			☐	☐	☐
			☐	☐	☐
			☐	☐	☐
			☐	☐	☐
			☐	☐	☐
			☐	☐	☐
			☐	☐	☐
			☐	☐	☐
			☐	☐	☐
			☐	☐	☐
			☐	☐	☐
			☐	☐	☐
			☐	☐	☐
			☐	☐	☐
			☐	☐	☐
			☐	☐	☐
			☐	☐	☐
			☐	☐	☐
			☐	☐	☐
			☐	☐	☐
			☐	☐	☐
			☐	☐	☐
			☐	☐	☐
			☐	☐	☐
			☐	☐	☐
			☐	☐	☐

Guest Lists

Name	Address	Phone	Status		
			Invited	RSVP	Thankyou
			☐	☐	☐
			☐	☐	☐
			☐	☐	☐
			☐	☐	☐
			☐	☐	☐
			☐	☐	☐
			☐	☐	☐
			☐	☐	☐
			☐	☐	☐
			☐	☐	☐
			☐	☐	☐
			☐	☐	☐
			☐	☐	☐
			☐	☐	☐
			☐	☐	☐
			☐	☐	☐
			☐	☐	☐
			☐	☐	☐
			☐	☐	☐
			☐	☐	☐
			☐	☐	☐
			☐	☐	☐
			☐	☐	☐
			☐	☐	☐
			☐	☐	☐
			☐	☐	☐

Guest Lists

Name	Address	Phone	Status		
			Invited	RSVP	Thankyou
			☐	☐	☐
			☐	☐	☐
			☐	☐	☐
			☐	☐	☐
			☐	☐	☐
			☐	☐	☐
			☐	☐	☐
			☐	☐	☐
			☐	☐	☐
			☐	☐	☐
			☐	☐	☐
			☐	☐	☐
			☐	☐	☐
			☐	☐	☐
			☐	☐	☐
			☐	☐	☐
			☐	☐	☐
			☐	☐	☐
			☐	☐	☐
			☐	☐	☐
			☐	☐	☐
			☐	☐	☐
			☐	☐	☐
			☐	☐	☐
			☐	☐	☐
			☐	☐	☐

Guest Lists

Name	Address	Phone	Status		
			Invited	RSVP	Thankyou
			☐	☐	☐
			☐	☐	☐
			☐	☐	☐
			☐	☐	☐
			☐	☐	☐
			☐	☐	☐
			☐	☐	☐
			☐	☐	☐
			☐	☐	☐
			☐	☐	☐
			☐	☐	☐
			☐	☐	☐
			☐	☐	☐
			☐	☐	☐
			☐	☐	☐
			☐	☐	☐
			☐	☐	☐
			☐	☐	☐
			☐	☐	☐
			☐	☐	☐
			☐	☐	☐
			☐	☐	☐
			☐	☐	☐
			☐	☐	☐
			☐	☐	☐
			☐	☐	☐

Guest Lists

Name	Address	Phone	Status		
			Invited	RSVP	Thankyou
			☐	☐	☐
			☐	☐	☐
			☐	☐	☐
			☐	☐	☐
			☐	☐	☐
			☐	☐	☐
			☐	☐	☐
			☐	☐	☐
			☐	☐	☐
			☐	☐	☐
			☐	☐	☐
			☐	☐	☐
			☐	☐	☐
			☐	☐	☐
			☐	☐	☐
			☐	☐	☐
			☐	☐	☐
			☐	☐	☐
			☐	☐	☐
			☐	☐	☐
			☐	☐	☐
			☐	☐	☐
			☐	☐	☐
			☐	☐	☐
			☐	☐	☐
			☐	☐	☐

Guest Lists

Name	Address	Phone	Status		
			Invited	RSVP	Thankyou
			☐	☐	☐
			☐	☐	☐
			☐	☐	☐
			☐	☐	☐
			☐	☐	☐
			☐	☐	☐
			☐	☐	☐
			☐	☐	☐
			☐	☐	☐
			☐	☐	☐
			☐	☐	☐
			☐	☐	☐
			☐	☐	☐
			☐	☐	☐
			☐	☐	☐
			☐	☐	☐
			☐	☐	☐
			☐	☐	☐
			☐	☐	☐
			☐	☐	☐
			☐	☐	☐
			☐	☐	☐
			☐	☐	☐
			☐	☐	☐
			☐	☐	☐
			☐	☐	☐

Guest Lists

Name	Address	Phone	Status		
			Invited	RSVP	Thankyou
			☐	☐	☐
			☐	☐	☐
			☐	☐	☐
			☐	☐	☐
			☐	☐	☐
			☐	☐	☐
			☐	☐	☐
			☐	☐	☐
			☐	☐	☐
			☐	☐	☐
			☐	☐	☐
			☐	☐	☐
			☐	☐	☐
			☐	☐	☐
			☐	☐	☐
			☐	☐	☐
			☐	☐	☐
			☐	☐	☐
			☐	☐	☐
			☐	☐	☐
			☐	☐	☐
			☐	☐	☐
			☐	☐	☐
			☐	☐	☐
			☐	☐	☐
			☐	☐	☐

Guest Lists

Name	Address	Phone	Status		
			Invited	RSVP	Thankyou
			☐	☐	☐
			☐	☐	☐
			☐	☐	☐
			☐	☐	☐
			☐	☐	☐
			☐	☐	☐
			☐	☐	☐
			☐	☐	☐
			☐	☐	☐
			☐	☐	☐
			☐	☐	☐
			☐	☐	☐
			☐	☐	☐
			☐	☐	☐
			☐	☐	☐
			☐	☐	☐
			☐	☐	☐
			☐	☐	☐
			☐	☐	☐
			☐	☐	☐
			☐	☐	☐
			☐	☐	☐
			☐	☐	☐
			☐	☐	☐
			☐	☐	☐
			☐	☐	☐

Table Seatings

Table Name.	No.

Table Name.	No.

Table Name.	No.

Table Name.	No.

Table Seatings

Table Name. No.

Table Name. No.

Table Name. No.

Table Name. No.

Table Seatings

Table Name. No.

Table Name. No.

Table Name. No.

Table Name. No.

Table Seatings

Table Name. No.

Table Name. No.

Table Name. No.

Table Name. No.

Table Seatings

Table Name. No.

Table Name. No.

Table Name. No.

Table Name. No.

Table Seatings

Table Name. No.

Table Name. No.

Table Name. No.

Table Name. No.

Table Seatings

Table Name. No.

Table Name. No.

Table Name. No.

Table Name. No.

Table Seatings

Table Name. No.

Table Name. No.

Table Name. No.

Table Name. No.

Table Seatings

Table Name. No.

Table Name. No.

Table Name. No.

Table Name. No.

Table Seatings

Table Name. No.

Table Name. No.

Table Name. No.

Table Name. No.

Song Lists

No.	Song Title	Ceromony Set	Notes

Song Lists

No.	Song Title	Ceromony Set	Notes

Menu Lists

Menu Lists

Menu Lists

Menu Lists

Rental Equipment

Rental Equipment

Honeymoon Planner

Details

Activity

Budget ________

Details	Cost
Total	

To Do List

- ○
- ○
- ○
- ○
- ○
- ○
- ○
- ○
- ○
- ○
- ○
- ○
- ○

Honeymoon Planner

Details

Activity

Budget ______________

Details	Cost
Total	

To Do List

- ○
- ○
- ○
- ○
- ○
- ○
- ○
- ○
- ○
- ○
- ○
- ○
- ○

Honeymoon Planner

Details

Activity

Budget ____________

Details	Cost
Total	

To Do List

- ○
- ○
- ○
- ○
- ○
- ○
- ○
- ○
- ○
- ○
- ○
- ○
- ○

Honeymoon Planner

Details

Activity

Budget ________________

Details	Cost
Total	

To Do List

- ○
- ○
- ○
- ○
- ○
- ○
- ○
- ○
- ○
- ○
- ○
- ○
- ○

To Do Lists

To Do Lists

To Do Lists

To Do Lists

To Do Lists

To Do Lists

To Do Lists

To Do Lists

To Do Lists

To Do Lists

Note

Note

Note

Note

Note

Note

Note

Note

Note

Note

Note

48073975R00064

Made in the USA
Middletown, DE
12 June 2019